I0136603

Frank Reynolds

The Jewish Monitor and Guide to the Holy Land

Frank Reynolds

The Jewish Monitor and Guide to the Holy Land

ISBN/EAN: 9783337102258

Printed in Europe, USA, Canada, Australia, Japan

Cover: Foto ©Lupo / pixelio.de

More available books at **www.hansebooks.com**

THE

JEWISH

MONITOR

AND

GUIDE

TO THE

Holy Land.

BY F. REYNOLDS.

HERALD BOOK AND JOB OFFICE.

THE

EWISH MONITOR

AND

GUIDE

TO THE

HOLY LAND.

———•—•———

Behold the days come, saith the Lord, that I will
perform that good thing which I have promised to
the house of Israel and the house of Judah.
   The secret things belong to the Lord our God
but those things which are revealed belong unto
us and to our children forever, that we may do all
the words of this law.—[BIBLE.

———•—•———

BY FRANK REYNOLDS.

———•—•———

HARLAN, IOWA.

HERALD BOOK AND JOB OFFICE.

Entered according to act of Congress. in the year 1877, by

FRANK REYNOLDS.

In the office of the Librarian of Congress, at Washington.

PREFACE.

The following pages contain a compilation of ancient prophecy, pointing out the present and future of the Jews and of Israel.

The purpose of the author is to place in the hands of the reader a MONITOR which, it is hoped, will be the means of diffusing light, not only among Hebrews but to all people, relative to Jehovah's purposes in the immediate future.

The renewal of the Jewish nation and the reorganizing of the tribes of Israel are particularly foreshadowed and carefully pointed out by the Prophets, who were made acquainted with God's purposes to the latest generation.

Believing that He Who foresaw and foretold the Babylonish captivity of 70 years duration, did also behold, through the vista of time, a much longer dispersion of his chosen people; and that he has foretold a great reunion at Jerusalem, which is made the burden of this small volume.

The ancient together with modern evidences of the return of the Jews to their own country are herein clearly set forth.

Due credit is given to historians and writers as well as recent travelers in the Holy Land, so far as known to the author.

Respectfully,

FRANK REYNOLDS.

JEWISH MONITOR

GUIDE TO THE HOLY LAND.

PART FIRST.

PRESENT AND FUTURE OF ISRAEL.

Remember the former things of old: for I am God, and there is none else; I am God, and there is none like me,

Declaring the end from the beginning, and from ancient times the things that are not yet done, saying, My counsel shall stand, and I will do all my pleasure: (Isaiah 46:9-10.

But ye, O mountains of Israel, ye shall shoot forth your branches, and yield your fruit to my people of Israel; for they are at hand to come.

For, behold I, am for you, and I will turn unto you, and ye shall be tilled and sown:

And I will multiply men upon you, all the house of Israel, even all of it: and the cities shall be inhabited, and the wastes shall be builded:

And I will multiply upon you man and beast; and they shall increase and bring fruit: and I will settle you after your old estates, and will do better unto you than at your beginnings: and ye shall know that I am the Lord. (Ezekiel 36:8-11).

The following recent history of the present situation of Palestine is very encouraging:

"It seems to be a well established fact that the last three or four years have witnessed a return of the Jews to Palestine from every quarter of the globe. The number going from Russia is entirely unprecedented. The Hebrew population of Jerusalem is more than double what it was ten years ago, and the movement is going on rapidly. Most of the city property is now in the hands of Jews, who have gone there from other countries, and in a few years' time they will probably be the owners of the whole city."

The speedy change wrought in Palestine has even astonished the wise of this age. In 1830 no visible change was witnessed different from that which had been common to that land for nearly eighteen centuries; but from 1830 to 1850, rain began to fall again in Palestine, and the ancient villages began to revive, and farms opened up; and in 1853 a surplus of fine wheat was sent to different parts—such a thing not having occurred for many centuries.

Fear not, O land; be glad and rejoice: for the Lord will do great things.

Be not afraid, ye beasts of the field: for the pastures of the wilderness do spring, for the tree beareth her fruit, the fig tree and the vine do yield their strength.

Be glad then, ye children of Zion, and rejoice in the Lord your God: for he hath given you the former rain moderately, and he will cause to come down for you the rain, the former rain, and the latter rain in the first month.

And the floors shall be full of wheat, and the fats shall overflow with the wine and oil.

And I will restore to you the years that the lo. cust hath eaten, the cankerworm, and the caterpil. lar, and the palmerworm, my great army I sent among you.

And ye shall eat in plenty, and be satisfied, and praise the name of the Lord your God, that hath dealt wondrously with you: and my people shall never be ashamed.

And ye shall know that I am in the midst of Israel, and that I am the Lord your God, and none else: and my people shall never be ashamed.

And it shall come to pass afterward, that I will pour out my Spirit upon all flesh; and your sons and your daughters shall prophesy, your old men shall dream dreams, your young men shall see visions:

And also upon the servants and upon the hand. maids in those days will I pour out my Spirit.

And I will shew wonders in the heavens and in the earth, blood, and fire, and pillars of smoke.

The sun shall be turned into darkness, and the moon into blood, before the great and the terrible day of the Lord come.

And it shall come to pass, that whosoever shall call on the name of the Lord shall be delivered: for in mount Zion and in Jerusalem shall be de. liverance, as the Lord hath said, and in the rem. nant whom the Lord shall call. (Joel 2:21-32).

The restoration of the abundant harvest of grain, fruit, etc., prior to God sending his "Spirit upon all flesh," is inevitable, and may we not make the application in these times?

"The result of Dr. Barclay's observations goes to show that the greatest fall of rain at Jerusalem in

a single year was eighty-five inches, and the small-
est forty-four, the mean being 51 1-6. These
figures will be best appreciated by recollecting
that the average rain-fall at London during the
whole year is only twenty-five inches, and that in
the wettest parts of the country, such as Cumber-
land and Devon, it rarely exceeds 50 inches. As
in the time of our Savior, (Luke 12:54), the rain
comes chiefly from the south, or southwest; they
commence at the end of October, or beginning of
November, and continue wthi greater or less con-
stancy till the end of February, or middle of March
and occasionally, though rarely, till the end of
April. Between April and November, there is,
with the rarest exception, an uninterrupted period
of fine weather, and skies without a cloud; during
the summer the dews are very heavy, and often
saturate the traveler's tent, as if a shower had
passed over it. The nights, especially towards
sunrise, are very cold, and thick fog or mists are
common all over the country. Thunder-storms
of great violence are frequent during the winter
months."

The following tabular statement of the fall of
rain between 1846 and 1853, as stated by Dr. Mac-
gowan, then residing at Jerusalem, will, doubtless, prove interesting:

RAIN-FALL IN JERUSALEM FROM 1846 TO 1853, IN INCHES,
ACCORDING TO NEWMAN'S RAIN-GAUGE.

Early Rains	1846-7	1847-8	1848-9	(*)	1850-1	1851-2	1852-3
Total....	20 1-5	43 3-5	35 3-5		54 4-5	28 4-5	15 3-5
Latter Rains.							
Total....	38 4-5	7 2-5	25		30 1-5	36 1-5	24 3-5

(*) 1849-0 not registered.

Thou shalt arise, and have mercy upon Zion:
for the time to favor her, yea, the set time is come.

For thy servants take pleasure in her stones, and
favor the dust thereof. (Psalms 102:13-14.)

To favor Zion, would be to fully organize her people upon the land consecrated to them for an everlasting possession. The following will represent the manner the organization will take place:

And their nobles shall be of themselves and their Governor shall proceed from the midst of them; and I will cause him to draw near, and he shall approach unto me: (Jer. 30:21.)

The Rev. Bonhomme says:

"Whatever opinion may be formed as to the special mode in which the attempts are made to restore the Jews to Palestine, the circumstances that the attention of so many individuals, Israelites and Christians as well as some of the crowned heads of Europe, has been called to the national prosperity of God's literal Israel, cannot be overlooked by the Hebrew Nation. In view of the Providential interference at this time, the Jews feel that they are no longer outcasts and despised, and they cannot remain indifferent to what is taking place.

Political changes are every year taking place in the East, which augur well for the Jews, and present appearances favor the expectations that further changes will soon so dispose the nations about Palestine, that the scattered millions of Israel may be restored to their native land.

The late projects of two eminent Jews, Rothschild and Sir Moses Montefiore, the first to purchase Jerusalem and its neighboring places, as a refuge and home to all Jews wishing to return to a land consecrated by a thousand sacred associations, and the latter to secure, by a sort of lease, the possession of several towns and villages held

sacred by the Jews, for the purpose of colonizing
them there, may indicate one means by which the
Jew may be reinstated into more than his original civil privileges.

    *   *   *   *   *   A party of wealthy
gentlemen from England left for Jerusalem, with
the purpose of commencing a colony in Jerico.
At Tyre and Sidon also, an architect from England
proceeded, with men and means, to commence a
colony.

An eminent Jew purchased land in the vicinity
of Jerusalem, and about Jaffa, upon which Jews
are settled and laboring. A wealthy Jewess, the
widow of a rich banker, Madame Polac, resident
at Kœnigsberg, Prussia, purchased the Mount of
Olives, in order to beautify the place with im-
provements at her own expense. The first thing
she did was to plant the whole area with a grove
of olive trees, and thus to restore it to the original
state of beauty from which it derives its name."

At the same time, saith the Lord, will I be the
God of all the families of Israel, and they shall
be my people.

Thus saith the Lord, The people which were
left of the sword found grace in the wilderness;
even Israel, when I went to cause him to rest.

The Lord hath appeared of old unto me, saying, Yea, I have loved thee with an· everlasting
love; therefore with loving-kindness have I drawn
thee.

Again I will build thee, and thou shalt be built,
O virgin of Israel: thou shalt again be adorned
with thy tabrets, and shalt go forth in the dances
of them that make merry.

Thou shalt yet plant vines upon the mountains
of Samaria: the planters shall plant, and shall eat
them as common things.

For there shall be a day, that the watchmen upon the mount Ephraim shall cry, Arise ye, and let us go up to Zion unto the Lord our God.

For thus saith the Lord; Sing with gladness for Jacob, and shout among the chief of the nations: publish ye, praise ye, and say, O Lord, save thy people, the remnant of Israel.

Behold, I will bring them from the north country, and gather them from the coasts of the earth, and with them the blind and the lame, the woman with child and her that travaileth with child together: a great company shall return thither.

They shall come with weeping, and with supplications will I lead them: I will cause them to walk by the rivers of waters in a straight way, wherein they shall not stumble; for I am a father to Israel, and Ephraim is my firstborn.

Hear the word of the Lord, O ye nations, and declare it in the isles afar off, and say, He that scattered Israel will gather him, and keep him, as a shepherd doth his flock.

For the Lord hath redeemed Jacob, and ransomed him from the hand of him that was stronger than he.

Therefore they shall come and sing in the height of Zion, and shall flow together to the goodness of the Lord, for wheat, and for wine, and for oil; and for the young of the flock and of the herd, and their soul shall be as a watered garden; and they shall not sorrow any more at all. (Jeremiah 31:1-12.)

The Rev. Bonhomme further says:

In turning our attention to the prospects of this people, we behold an ever-active Providence in preparing the way for restoring his chosen nation to the land of their fathers, and to the favor of their God, and to the beloved, their Messiah,

Prince and King. The time is near at hand when this standing monument of Divine displeasure, this once highly honored but now scattered and dispersed family, is to be gathered from all the nations whither the Lord their God has scattered them.

When this period shall have come—come it must—it will be an eventful period for the world. (Micah 7:18-20.) The Prophet, anticipating their restoration, says: "An highway shall be made for them, as in the days of Assyria, when they came up out of the land of Egypt." When this people went down into Egypt, the Assyrian oppressed them. When the Lord was about to deliver them, he called Moses, the man of God, and said unto him, "I have seen the affliction of my people, and am come down to deliver them."—Every difficulty was taken out of the way, and they went out triumphantly. In like manner, when the seventy years of Babylon's captivity had expired, the Lord inclined the hearts of Darius and Cyrus, by whose decrees in their favor every hindrance was removed for their return to their own beloved land. In fact, the only plan which would tend to effectually secure the peace and prosperity of Palestine, would be the settlement of the many millions of them there; being an active, enterprising people, they would soon rid the land of the marauding Arab tribes and promote its welfare in every respect.

Recent discoveries made in Africa and Japan, among the Affghans and Chinese, will swell the number greatly. Having taken special pains within the last twenty years to collect carefully from missionary statistics furnished by the missionaries sent among the Jews throughout the world—missionaries numbering between two hun-

dred and three hundred—a source most reliable—
the following is a table, in specified order, as to
the actual number of Jews scattered:

China, including Ka-Fung-fu.	60,000
Russian Provinces in Asia.	3,000
Russia proper	1,200,000
Poland	2,000,000
Prussia proper	135,000
Austria	453,524
Confederate States of Germany.	138,000
Amsterdam, in Holland	35,000
The Netherlands.	50,000
France	81,000
Italy	200,000
England	60,000
Ionian Isles	7,000
Danish States	15,000
Sweden	1,700
Switzerland	1,900
Gibralter	4,000
Galatia	200,000
Netherlandish Colonies	500
Kingstown, West Indies	5,000
Demarara, Esquibo.	200
New Holland	50
St. Domingo,	5,000
Porto Rico.	3,300
United States	700,000
South America.	10,000
Fez, in Africa and Morocco,	300,000
Tunis	130,000
Algiers	30.000
Habesh.	20,000
Tripoli.	12,000
Egypt,	12,000
In the Turkish Dominions in Europe and Asia	2,500,000

Those discovered in the East, as mentioned in 2 Kings 17:6, the original country where the ten tribes were carried away captive, the identified ten tribes of which we have a complete history of recent dates.............. 7,000.000

A grand total of............... 15,000,000

And their seed shall be known among the Gentiles, and their offspring among the people: all that see them shall acknowledge them, that they are the seed which the Lord hath blessed. (Isaiah 61:9.)

That Jews are known, wherever the sun shines, is true: And when it is known that Jehovah appears once more in their defense upon the mountains of Israel, all people will have to acknowledge the unexpected favor extended to them.

Lift up thine eyes round about, and behold: all these gather themselves together and come to thee. As I live, saith the Lord, thou shalt surely clothe thee with them all, as with an ornament, and bind them on thee, as a bride doeth.

For thy waste and thy desolate places, and the land of thy destruction, shall even now be too narrow by reason of the inhabitants, and they that swallowed thee up shall be far away.

The children which thou shalt have, after thou hast lost the other, shall say again in thine ears, The place is too strait for me: give place to me that I may dwell.

Then shalt thou say in thine heart, Who hath begotten me these, seeing I have lost my children, and am desolate, a captive, and removing to and fro? and who hath brought up these? Behold, I was left alone; these, where had they been?

Thus saith the Lord God, Behold, I will lift up mine hand to the Gentiles, and set up my standard to the people: and they shall bring thy sons in their arms, and thy daughters shall be carried upon their shoulders.

And kings shall be thy nursing fathers, and their queens thy nursing mothers: they shall bow down to thee with their face toward the earth, and lick up the dust of thy feet; and thou shalt know that I am the Lord: for they shall not be ashamed that wait for me. (Isaiah 49:18–23.)

"Among the signs of the times may be noted a fact which will interest many Christians. The Rev. James Neil, an English clergyman who has lived for some time in Jerusalem, has written a book, in which he says that the Jews are returning in large numbers to Palestine. So great is the influx of new-comers, chiefly Jews from Russia, that the population of Palestine has doubled within the last ten years.

At Laphed, one of the four holy cities of Galilee, there was, three years ago, so large an emigration that many of the immigrants had to camp out, the houses being insufficient to contain them.

Building goes on in Jerusalem in the night as well as in the day, and a plot of ground near the city has been sold for twenty times its former price. The apparent causes of this migration are first, that now Jews are permitted to own land in Palestine without becoming Turkish subjects; and secondly, the new law in Russia (1874) which compels all Jews to be enrolled for military service."

Behold, I will gather them out of all countries, whither I have driven them in mine anger, and

In my fury, and in great wrath; and I will bring
them again unto this place, and I will cause them
to dwell safely:

And they shall be my people, and I will be
their God:

And I will give them one heart, and one way,
that they may fear me for ever, for the good of
them, and of their children after them:

And I will make an everlasting covenant with
them, that I will not turn away from them, to do
them good; but I will put my fear in their hearts,
that they shall not depart from me.

Yea, I will rejoice over them to do them good,
and I will plant them in this land assuredly with
my whole heart and with my whole soul.

For thus saith the Lord; Like as I have brought
all this great evil upon this people, so will I bring
upon them all the good that I have promised them.

And fields shall be bought in this land, where-
of ye say, It is desolate without man or beast; it
is given into the hand of the Chaldeans.

Men shall buy fields for money, and subscribe
evidences, and seal them, and take witnesses in
the land of Benjamin, and in the places about Jerusalem, and in the cities of Judah, and in the
cities of the mountains, and in the cities of the
valley, and in the cities of the south: for I will
cause their captivity to return, saith the Lord.—
Jer. 32:37–44.)

"Sir Moses Montefiore, now in the 92d year of
his age, a few months back paid a seventh visit
to Jerusalem for the purpose of collecting infor-
mation relating to the actual condition of the
Jewish inhabitants of the Holy Land, as to their
capability and inclination to engage in mechan-
ical and general agricultural pursuits. The report
(the London Times says) is now published, with

a letter to Sir Moses from two of the leading Rabbies of Jerusalem, in which they refute the charges of disinclination to work of the Jews of Jerusalem while there was a possibility of obtaining sufficient charity to enable them to live. It is known that, in order to give a refutation to these charges, Sir Moses Montefiore determined to undertake a mission to the Holy City and report on his observations. Sir Moses states that a whole village has been pointed out to him which might be purchased at a moderate rate. All the persons who reported to Sir Moses on this subject stated that there would be no difficulty whatever in securing as much land as might be required, either for cultivation or building purposes. The Governor and Kadi of Jerusalem assured him of the readiness of the Turkish Government to render every possible assistance to encourage any industrial scheme for the promotion of the welfare of the people in the Holy Land. The French and American Consuls also assured him of their willingness to assist. Sir Moses states that a great struggle may arrise in the future between the educated or Progressive party—those who do not come to the Holy City from religious motives, but from reasons connected with special circumstances—and the strictly conservative party, whose sole object in going to Jerusalem was the preservation of their religion. During his short stay at Jaffa, Sir Moses Montefiore noticed some indications to that effect. Sir Moses gives a long account of the different institutions established in Jerusalem for the benefit of the poor. There is a soup kitchen; a loan society, whose object it is to make advances without interest; a hospice, which provides every poor person coming to Jerusalem with gratuitous board and lodging until he may have procured for himself a suitable residence; three building societies, etc. Sir Moses says: "I had some conversation on the subject of general drainage in Jerusalem with a gentleman of authority. He told me that all the refuse of the city is now carried into the pool of Bethesda, which, strange to say, I was informed, is close to the house intended for the barracks, and the soldiers living there appear not to experience the least inconvenience on account of its vicinity. If arrangements could be made to clear that pool entirely, to admit pure water only, and to dig special pools for the purpose of conducting there the city drains, Jerusalem might become free from any threatening epidemic. All the doctors in Jerusalem assured me that the Holy City might be reckoned, on account of the purity of the atmosphere, one of the healthiest of places." Sir Moses speaks of the skill of Jewish mechanics in Jerusalem, where it has been said that there are no Jewish mechanics in the Holy City. Sir Moses saw watchmakers, engravers, lithographers, sculptors, goldsmiths, bookbinders and carpenters, and, he says, "all did their work most satisfactorily." A watchmaker into whose hands he gave a valuable repeater for repair, put it within a very short time, into excellent order. The same man, in addition to his skill as a watchmaker, displayed also great talent as a Hebrew caligraphist. He presented Sir Moses with a grain of wheat on which were written nineteen lines, forming an acrostic on the name of the venerable philanthropist. The traveler states that he has had every opportunity of convincing himself that the Jews are eager and willing to engage in any kind of labor, agricultural or otherwise, which will obtain for them the necessaries of life and place them above the need of the charity of their benevolent co-religionists. Sir Moses says that the great regard which he has always entertained toward his brethren in the Holy Land has now become, if possible, doubly increased, and he emphatically asserts that they are deserving of assistance; they are willing and able to work, their mental powers are of a satisfactory nature, and all Israelites ought to render them support."

And it shall come to pass, when all these things are come upon thee, the blessing and the curse, which I have set before thee, and shalt call them to mind among all the nations, whither the Lord thy God hath driven thee,

And shalt return unto the Lord thy God, and shalt obey his voice according to all that I command thee this day, thou and thy children, with all thine heart, and with all thy soul;

That then the Lord thy God will turn thy captivity, and have compassion upon thee, and will return and gather thee from all the nations, whither the Lord thy God hath scattered thee.

If any of thine be driven out unto the outmost parts of heaven, from thence will the Lord thy God gather thee, and from thence will he fetch thee:

And the Lord thy God will bring thee into the land which thy fathers possessed, and thou shalt possess it; and he will do thee good, and multiply thee above thy fathers. (Deut. 30:1–5.)

Col. J. P. Sanford, a recent traveler in China, Egypt and Palestine, now lecturing in the United States upon what he saw abroad, states that fruit grows in abundance in Palestine; that he saw grapes that weighed seven pounds to the bunch and that bunches generally ranged from four to ten pounds each: That Jews were emigrating there from all parts of the world, and when they arrived much time was first spent in "prayer and wailing," beseeching God to bless and renew their land by his omnipotent hand saying, "how long O Lord, until thou wilt favor again our desolate homes?"

In that day will I raise up the tabernacle of David that is fallen, and close up the breaches thereof: and I will raise up his ruins, and I will build it as in the days of old:

That they may possess the remnant of Edom, and of all the heathen, which are called by my name, saith the Lord that doeth this.

Behold, the days come, saith the Lord, that the ploughman shall overtake the reaper, and the treader of grapes him that soweth seed; and the mountains shall drop sweet wine, and all the hills shall melt.

And I will bring again the captivity of my people of Israel, and they shall build the waste cities, and inhabit them; and they shall plant vineyards, and drink the wine thereof; they shall also make gardens, and eat the fruit of them.

And I will plant them upon their land, and they shall no more be pulled up out of their land which I have given them, saith the Lord thy God.— (Amos 9:11-15.)

The following is from a recent traveler in that country of my acquaintance:

"I arrived in Indiana a few days since, from the Eastern Continent. I stopped at Joppa nearly the whole winter. For my part I was well pleased with the country, it is certainly a land of most wonderful fruitfulness, with a delightsome climate, producing everything if properly cultivated, and from two to three crops in a year. They have grain, fruit and vegetables all the year round; in fact I never was in such a country before. I have seen much good country in Europe and America, but none to compare with Palestine; its fruitfulness is uncommon, and the climate the most delightsome; even in winter I did not see the least sort of frost, and vegetables of every sort were growing in perfection in gardens. It is a fact that the rain and dew are restored; recently, in 1853, the former and the latter rains were restored, to the astonishment of the natives. The Jews have been returning to the Holy Land for some time, and are increasing, going to their beloved Canaan from many parts of Europe, Asia and Africa.— They are making preparations to rebuild cities and build railroads. The fruit in Palestine is better than in Europe and America. They have camels, mules, horses, asses, cattle, sheep and goats; but I saw no hogs. The natives are generally friendly."

The sons also of them that afflicted thee shall come bending unto thee; and all they that despised thee shall bow themselves down at the soles of thy feet; and they shall call thee, The city of the Lord, The Zion of the Holy One of Israel.

Whereas thou hast been forsaken and hated, so that no man went through thee; I will make thee an eternal excellency, a joy of many generations.

Thou shalt also suck the milk of the Gentiles, and shalt suck the breast of kings: and thou shalt know that I the Lord am thy Saviour and thy Redeemer, the Mighty One of Jacob.

For brass I will bring gold, and for iron I will bring silver, and for wood brass, and for stones iron: I will also make thy officers peace, and thine exactors righteousness. (Isaiah 60:14–17).

The Lord has always worked by means, and often used the basest of men to perform his determined purposes: For instance, Cyrus, a heathen king, was even named two hundred years before he was born, as being the one to restore Israel from Babylonish captivity to their own land.

Who are they that now fear the future changes? They are the nations with whom abide the wealthy Israelites: The abundance of the precious metals will be brought up from some quarter, and the entire globe will feel the effects of its transit; but will they remember that God is at the helm?

For I know their works and their thoughts: it shall come, that I will gather all nations and tongues; and they shall come, and see my glory.

And I will set a sign among them and I will send those that escape of them unto the nations, to Tarshish, Pul, and Lud, that draw the bow, to Tubal and Javan, to the isles afar off, that have not heard my fame, neither have seen my glory; and they shall declare my glory among the Gentiles.

And they shall bring all your brethren for an offering unto the Lord out of all nations upon horses, and in chariots, and in litters, and upon mules, and upon swift beasts, to my holy mountain Jerusalem, saith the Lord, as the children of Israel bring an offering in a clean vessel into the house of the Lord.

And I will also take of them for priests and for Levites, saith the Lord.

For as the new heavens, and the new earth,

which I will make, shall remain before me, saith
the Lord, so shall your seed and your name remain. (Isaiah 66:18–22).

By what power, or means, God will "Set a sign
among the nations," I do not propose to conjec-
ture, further than the Bible will warrant. Amos
tells us how God works:

Surely the Lord God will do nothing, but he
revealeth his secret unto his servants the prophets. (Amos 3:7).

The prophets come from the house of Israel.—
God has never raised up a prophet outside of
Abraham's seed since the promise was bestowed
upon him, viz: "That in thee and in thy seed shall
all the nations of the Earth be blessed." Neither
has God ever promised to raise up a prophet
among the Gentiles: Hence, since the dissolving
of the Jewish nation, darkness, even "Gross darkness" has covered the people.

O Lord, why hast thou made us to err from thy
ways, and hardened our heart from thy fear? Return for thy servants' sake, the tribes of thine inheritance.

The people of thy holiness have possessed it but
a little while: our adversaries have trodden
down thy sanctuary.

We are thine: thou never barest rule over them;
they were not called by thy name. (Isa. 63:17-19.)

Declare ye in Judah, and publish in Jerusalem;
and say, Blow ye the trumpet in the land: cry,
gather together, and say, Assemble yourselves and
let us go into the defenced cities.

Set up the standard toward Zion: retire, stay

not: for I will bring evil from the north, and a
great destruction.

The lion is come up from his thicket, and the
destroyer of the Gentiles is on his way; he is gone
forth from his place to make thy land desolate;
and thy cities shall be laid waste, without an inhabitant. (Jer. 4:5–7).

The following, from the "Christian Union," re-
veals the position of thousands of the Hebrew
people in past centuries:

Just now, both in this country and in Europe,
there is what we may call an epidemic of the
Jewish question.   Here, as well as there, the dis-
cussion is but the rebound of circumstances.   Mr.
Disraeli was thought to have drawn upon his very
opulent oriental imagination when he stated, some
years ago, that in all parts of the world there
were Jews, who, shrinking from the excruciating
contempt and aversion of mankind, concealed
their faith, not only for a life-time, but for generations.   Some facts have lately come to the sur-
face which indicate that Disraeli knew what he
was talking about.   For example, it is mentioned
in a recent number of the "Jewish Chronicle,"
that a company of Jews at Berlin brought to the
Shah, on the occasion of the latter's visit there, a
petition imploring him to protect the Jews in Per-
sia; and that a stern Persian, belonging to the
Royal Suit, who had received and closely ques-
tioned the delegation, quietly informed them that
their memorial should really reach the Shah, for
he, the stern Persian aforesaid, was a concealed
Jew, though obliged to deny his faith.   Since the
religious emancipation of Austria and Spain,
there have been numerous conversions to Judaism, which were in reality nothing more than the

open avowal of Judaism by "Catholic" families who perhaps for ages, have remained Jews in sympathy and faith and domestic habits, while they have outwardly assented to the dominant and domineering religion.

And I will cause the captivity of Judah and the captivity of Israel to return, and will build them, as at the first.

And I will cleanse them from all their iniquity, whereby they have sinned against me; and I will pardon all their iniquities, whereby they have sinned, and whereby they have transgressed against me.

And it shall be to me a name of joy, a praise and an honour before all the nations of the earth, which shall hear all the good that I do unto them: and they shall fear and tremble for all the goodness and for all the prosperity that I procure unto it.

Thus saith the Lord; Again there shall be heard in this place, which ye say shall be desolate without man and without beast, even in the cities of Judah, and in the streets of Jerusalem, that are desolate, without man, and without inhabitant, and without beast,

The voice of joy, and the voice of gladness, the voice of the bridegroom, and the voice of the bride, the voice of them that shall say, Praise the Lord of hosts: for the Lord is good; for his mercy endureth for ever: and of them that shall bring the sacrifice of praise into the house of the Lord. For I will cause to return the captivity of the land, as at the first, saith the Lord.

Thus saith the Lord of hosts; Again in this place, which is desolate without man and without beast, and in all the cities thereof, shall be a habitation of shepherds causing their flocks to lie down.

In the cities of the mountains, in the cities of the vale, and in the cities of the south, and in the land of Benjamin, and in the places about Jerusalem, and in the cities of Judah, shall the flocks pass again under the hands of him that telleth them, saith the Lord.

. Behold, the days come, saith the Lord, that I will perform that good thing which I have promised unto the house of Israel and to the house of Judah.

In those days, and at that time, will I cause the Branch of righteousness to grow up unto David; and he shall execute judgment and righteousness in the land.

In those days shall Judah be saved, and Jerusalem shall dwell safely: and this is the name wherewith she shall be called, The Lord our Righteousness.

For thus saith the Lord; David shall never want a man to sit upon the throne of the house of Israel: (Jer. 33:7-17).

The days in which Judah shall be saved will be when the New Era has come: The time which the prophets have all spoken of since the world began—even of the "restoration of all things," and when this time shall have come, the ancient date for reckoning time will end, and the throne of David will never be in want of a King, under the new dispensation spoken of in the above prophecy.

Thus saith the Lord God; In the day that I shall have cleansed you from all your iniquities I will also cause you to dwell in the cities, and the wastes shall be builded.

And the desolate land shall be tilled, whereas it lay desolate in the sight of all that passed by.

And they shall say, This land that was desolate is become like the garden of Eden; and the waste and desolate and ruined cities are become fenced, and are inhabited.

Then the heathen that are left round about you shall know that I the Lord build the ruined places, and plant that that was desolate: I the Lord have spoken it, and I will do it.

Thus saith the Lord God; I will yet for this be inquired of by the house of Israel, to do it for them; I will increase them with men like a flock.

As the holy flock, as the flock of Jerusalem in her solemn feasts; so that the waste cities be filled with flocks of men: and they shall know that I am the Lord. (Ezekiel 36:33–38).

We annex the following testimony:

"An important society has been formed in Europe, called the International Society of the Orient, to prevent the grave complications arising out of the Eastern Question and to regenerate the East, by infusing therein the spirit of western civilization. To accomplish this great result, the Society, which enrolls among its members, such men as Napoleon, Rothchilds, and Montefiore, proposes to favor the development of agriculture, industry, commerce, and public works in the East, especially in Palestine; to obtain from the Turkish government certain privileges and monopolies, chief of which is the gradual concession and advancement of the lands of Palestine; to distribute at cash prices such of those lands as the company receives, and to effect the colonization of the most fertile villages of the Holy Land. The Society, after having established its commercial

bureau at Constantinople and other cities of the
Turkish empire, will construct a port at Joppa,
and a good road, or railroad, from that city to Jerusalem. Upon the north of this road, the Society expects land to be conceded by Turkey, which
they will sell to Israelitish families.' These, in
their turn, will create new colonies, aided by their
Oriental co-religionists, and it is expected special
committees will send thither Jews of Morocco,
Poland, Moldavia, Wallachia, from the East,
and from Africa. The society claims that the plan
will reconstruct the holy places of Jerusalem in
a Christian manner, put an end to the constant
conflict between the great powers in reference to
them, transform the ancient Jerusalem into a new
and great city, create European colonies, which
will become, in time, the centers, whence Occi-
dental civilization will spread in Turkey and pen-
etrate to the remote Orient. The Society is being
rapidly formed, with the strongest influences,
financial and political at its back. The Rothchilds, Mores, Montefiore, and other great capi-
talists among the Jews, are actively in sympathy
with the undertaking. The plan has also the favor of more than one crowned head in Europe;
amongst them, Napoleon, of whose special theo-
ries of nationalities it is a development. Several
prominent noblemen of England, and the leading
names of the Faubourg St. Germain are also
among its friends."

And therefore will the Lord wait, that he may
be gracious unto you, and therefore will he be exalted, that he may have mercy upon you: for the
Lord is a God of judgment: blessed are all they
that wait for him.

For the people shall dwell in Zion at Jerusalem: thou shalt weep no more: he will be very

gracious unto thee at the voice of thy cry; when he shall hear it, he will answer thee.

And though the Lord give you the bread of adversity, and the water of affliction, yet shall not thy teachers be removed into a corner any more, but thine eyes shall see thy teachers:

And thine ears shall hear a word behind thee, saying, This is the way, walk ye in it, when ye turn to the right hand, and when ye turn to the left. (Isaiah 30:18-21).

Daniel March, D. D., utters the following noble and truthful statement:

Under the Divine guidance the men who made the deepest impress upon the life of the world, were not the men who founded cities, and conquered nations, and governed empires, but the pilgrims and wanderers who dwelt in tents and found in the Almighty God their shield and exceeding great reward. We cannot point to fallen columns, and ruined temples, and desolate cities and say: These are the works of our father Abraham. But we can find his living memorial in the life and character of the best and bravest men of all succeeding time. * * Moses lived eighty years in the desert, and his only home was a tent. And Yet these two mighty men of faith are still monarchs in the realm of mind, friends and fathers in the sacred empire of home.

For Zion,s sake will I not hold my peace, and for Jerusalem's sake I will not rest, until the righteousness thereof go forth as brightness, and the salvation thereof as a lamp that burneth.

And the Gentiles shall see thy righteousness, and all kings thy glory: and thou shalt be called by a new name, which the mouth of the Lord shall name.

Thou shalt also be a crown of glory in the hand of the Lord, and a royal diadem in the hand of thy God.

Thou shalt no more be termed Forsaken; neither shall thy land any more be termed Desolate: but thou shalt be called Hephzibah, and thy land Beulah: for the Lord delighteth in thee, and thy land shall be married.

For as a young man marrieth a virgin, so shall thy sons marry thee: and as the bridegroom rejoiceth over the bride, so shall thy God rejoice over thee.

I have set watchmen upon thy walls, O Jerusalem, which shall never hold their peace day nor night: ye that make mention of the Lord, keep not silence,

And give him no rest, till he establish, and till he make Jerusalem a praise in the earth.

The Lord hath sworn by his right hand, and by the arm of his strength, Surely I will no more give thy corn to be meat for thine enemies; and the sons of the stranger shall not drink thy wine, for the which thou hast laboured:

But they that have gathered it shall eat it, and praise the Lord; and they that have brought it together shall drink it in the courts of my holiness.

Go through, go through the gates; prepare ye the way of the people; cast up, cast up the highway; gather out the stones; lift up a standard for the people.

Behold, the Lord hath proclaimed unto the end of the world, Say ye to the daughter of Zion, Behold, thy salvation cometh; behold, his reward is with him, and his work before him.

And they shall call them, The holy people, The redeemed of the Lord: and thou shalt be called, Sought out, A city not forsaken. (Isa. 62:1–12).

"Palestine is not such a desert as some people suppose. Even after the waste and exhaustion of 4000 years it exhibits surprising fertility. The hill country of Galilee yields crops which indicate a production equal to all that Josephus has said of it. South of Bethlehem they raise two crops a year. Their grapes almost rival the clusters of Eshcol, a single vine having 100 bunches of grapes, each three feet long and each grape three and one half inches in circumference. They have Indian corn eleven feet high. Water-melons twenty, thirty, and forty pounds weight, and bean pods thirteen inches long and six on a stem.— Their quince-trees yield 400 quinces each, which are larger than the largest apples of New England, and a single citron-tree yields 510 pounds of fruit."

I lifted up mine eyes again, and looked, and behold a man with a measuring line in his hand.

Then said I, Whither goest thou? And he said unto me, To measure Jerusalem, to see what is the breadth thereof, and what is the length thereof.

And, behold, the angel that talked with me went forth, and another angel went out to meet him,

And said unto him, Run, speak to this young man, saying, Jerusalem shall be inhabited as towns without walls for the multitude of men and cattle therein:

For I, saith the Lord, will be unto her a wall of fire round about, and will be the glory in the midst of her.

Ho, ho, come forth, and flee from the land of the north, saith the Lord: for I have spread you abroad as the four winds of the heaven, saith the Lord.

Deliver thyself, O Zion, that dwellest with the daughter of Babylon.

For thus saith the Lord of hosts; After the glory hath he sent me unto the nations which spoiled you: for he that toucheth you, toucheth the apple of his eye.

For, behold, I Will shake mine hand upon them, and they shall be a spoil to their servants: and ye shall know that the Lord of hosts hath sent me.

Sing and rejoice, O daughter of Zion: for, lo, I come, and I will dwell in the midst of thee, saith the Lord.

And many nations shall be joined to the Lord in that day, and shall be my people: and I will dwell in the midst of thee, and thou shalt know that the Lord of hosts hath sent me unto thee.

And the Lord shall inherit Judah his portion in the holy land, and shall choose Jerusalem again.

Be silent, O all flesh, before the Lord: for he is raised up out of his holy habitation. (Zechariah 2:1-13).

To protect the city of Jerusalem, in past ages, a wall was erected; but the weapons of war now used, demand something more efficient: God has promised to be a defense in the age of Israel's victory and redemption.

In that day will I make the governors of Judah like a hearth of fire among the wood, and like a torch of fire in a sheaf; and they shall devour all the people round about, on the right hand and on the left: and Jerusalem shall be inhabited again in her own place, even in Jerusalem.

The Lord also shall save the tents of Judah first, that the glory of the house of David and the glory of the inhabitants of Jerusalem do not magnify themselves against Judah.

In that day shall the Lord defend the inhabitants
of Jerusalem; and he that is feeble among them
at that day shall be as David; and the house of
David shall be as God, as the angel of the Lord
before them.

And it shall come to pass in that day, that I will
seek to destroy all the nations that come against
Jerusalem. (Zech. 12:5-9).

Come, behold the works of the Lord, what des-
olations he hath made in the earth.   ⸱

He maketh wars to cease unto the end of the
earth; he breaketh the bow, and cutteth the spear
in sunder; he burneth the chariot in the fire.

Be still, and know that I am God: I will be exalted among the heathen, I will be exalted in the
earth.

The Lord of hosts is with us; the God of Jacob
is our refuge. Selah. (Psalms 46:8-11).

Behold, the days come, saith the Lord, that I
will make a new covenant with the house of Israel, and with the house of Judah:

Not according to the covenant that I made with
their fathers, in the day that I took them by the
hand to bring them out of the land of Egypt;
which my covenant they break, although I was a
husband unto them, saith the Lord:

But this shall be the covenant that I will make
with the house of Israel: After those days, saith
the Lord, I will put my law in their inward parts,
and write it in their hearts; and will be their
God, and they shall be my people.

And they shall teach no more every man his
neighbour, and every man his brother, saying,
Know the Lord: for they shall all know me, from
the least of them unto the greatest of them, saith
the Lord: for I will forgive their iniquity, and I
will remember their sin no more.

Thus saith the Lord, which giveth the sun for a light by day, and the ordinances of the moon and of the stars for a light by night, which divideth the sea when the waves thereof roar; The Lord of hosts is his name:

If those ordinances depart from before me, saith the Lord, then the seed of Israel also shall cease from being a nation before me for ever.

Thus saith the Lord; If heaven above can be measured, and the foundations of the earth searched out beneath, I will also cast off all the seed of Israel for all that they have done, saith the Lord.

Behold, the days come, saith the Lord, that the city shall be built to the Lord from the tower of Hananeel unto the gate of the corner.

And the measuring line shall yet go forth over against it upon the hill Gareb, and shall compass about to Goath.

And the whole valley of the dead bodies, and of the ashes, and all the field unto the brook of Kidron, unto the corner of the horse gate toward the east, shall be holy unto the Lord; it shall not be plucked up, nor thrown down any more for ever. (Jer. 31:31–40).

The Covenant alluded to in the above, was never made with Israel and Judah; it is a different agreement from that made under the direction of Moses in the exodus from Egypt. In the new covenant, all are to become acquainted with God No teachers will be required; hence, we need not expect to find this covenant on earth at the present time, for the world is encumbered with teachers; and I must say (will the reader dissent?) that the following, clipped from "Spirit of the Times," is only an echo from the dark ages from which we are not fully recovered; and were it not for the faithful Hebrews, how much would the present generation know of Jehovah:

A young minister had gone to a prosperous church to preach his first sermon. Before leaving the house the gentleman who was entertaining him suggested to him not to preach against the Universalists. "There are," said he, "several Universalist families who have pews in our church, and we don't want them offended." The young minister promised. At the church vestibule one of the deacons drew him aside, and said, "Do you see those gentlemen just passing in? They are Spiritualists, but come here to church occasionally. I wish you would be a little careful not to say anything that might hurt their feelings." The minister promised. As he was ascending the pulpit steps, one of the elders button-holed him for a moment to whisper an additional caution— "The leading liquor dealer has just come into the church, and he gives us a lift sometimes. I wish you would be particular not to allude to the whisky business or the temperance question." The young minister, getting fairly frightened to see the moral ground thus steadily narrowing before him, inquired, "Pray, who or what shall I preach against, then?" The elder's reply came with an air of triumph—"Preach against the Jews; they haven't got a friend in town."

The wilderness and the solitary place shall be glad for them; and the desert shall rejoice, and blossom as the rose.

It shall blossom abundantly, and rejoice even,

with joy and singing: the glory of Lebanon shall be given unto it, the excellency of Carmel and Sharon; they shall see the glory of the Lord, and the excellency of our God.

Strengthen ye the weak hands, and confirm the feeble knees.

Say to them that are of a fearful heart, Be strong, fear not: behold, your God will come with vengeance, even God with a recompense; he will come and save you.

Then the eyes of the blind shall be opened, and the ears of the deaf shall be unstopped.

Then shall the lame man leap as a hart, and the tongue of the dumb sing: for in the wilderness shall waters break out, and streams in the desert.

And the parched ground shall become a pool, and the thirsty land springs of water: in the habitation of dragons, where each lay, shall be grass with reeds and rushes.

And a highway shall be there, and a way, and it shall be called The way of holiness; the unclean shall not pass over it; but it shall be for those: the wayfaring men, though fools, shall not err therein.

No lion shall be there, nor any ravenous beast shall go up thereon, it shall not be found there; but the redeemed shall walk there:

And the ransomed of the Lord shall return, and come to Zion with songs and everlasting joy upon their heads: they shall obtain joy and gladness, and sorrow and sighing shall flee away. (Isaiah 35:1-10).

The following, which we quote from the "Jewish Times," published in New York, favors the Colonization of Palestine:

Sir Moses Montefiore, the venerable advocate of the Jews, has issued a circular letter urging the

colonization of Palestine and the encouragement
of Jewish agriculturists and mechanics. The
project seems by no means impracticable. Whatever opinion people of a liberal turn of mind may
entertain regarding the veneration due to the ancient home of the Jews, there can be no doubt
entertained that millions of Jews look upon Palestine as the land holy par excellence, the place
nearest to the future abode of bliss, and in direct
connection with the Paradise of Saints. An irre-
pressible desire and burning longing dwell in
the breasts of thousands of our brethren for the
land which, in their opinion, is alone worthy to
contain the temple for the worship of the true
God, and where they may best secure the due
preparation for entering the home of eternity.

Therefore, behold, the days come, saith the
Lord, that it shall no more be said, The Lord liveth, that brought up the children of Israel out of
the land of Egypt;

But, The Lord liveth, that brought up the children of Israel from the land of the north, and
from all the lands whither he had driven them:
and I will bring them again into their land that I
gave unto their fathers.

Behold, I will send for many fishers, saith the
Lord, and they shall fish them; and after will I
send for many hunters, and they shall hunt them
from every mountain, and from every hill, and
out of the holes of the rocks.

For mine eyes are upon all their ways: they are
not hid from my face, neither is their iniquity hid
from mine eyes.

And first I will recompense their iniquity and
their sin double; because they have defiled my
land, they have filled mine inheritance with the

carcasses of their detestable and abominable things.

O Lord, my strength, and my fortress, and my refuge in the day of affliction, the Gentiles shall come unto thee from the ends of the earth, and shall say, Surely our fathers have inherited lies, vanity, and things wherein there is no profit.— (Jer. 16:14–19).

When the promises of God to the Hebrews are beginning to be made manifest again, the Gentiles will doubt the correctness of their long cherished belief, that God has cast the Jews off forever. I will here say that many good men believe in the literal return of Israel to their promised land.

Rev. Charles Wesley, a great reformer, who frequently expressed his feeling and belief on his subject furnishes the following:

> Almighty God of love,
>   Set up the attracting sign,
> And summon whom thou dost approve
>   For messengers divine.

> From favored Abram's seed,
>   The new Apostles choose;
> In Isles and Continents to spread,
>   The Dead-reviving news.

> We know it shall be done!
>   'Tis God's almighty word;
> All Israel shall the Messiah own,
>   To their first state restored.

PART SECOND.

ISRAEL'S FINAL REDEMPTION.

Behold, I will send my messenger, and he shall prepare the way before me: and the Lord, whom ye seek, shall suddenly come to his temple, even the messenger of the covenant, whom ye delight in: behold, he shall come, saith the Lord of hosts.

But who may abide the day of his coming? and who shall stand when he appeareth? for he is like a refiner's fire, and like fullers' soap:

And he shall sit as a refiner and purifier of silver: and he shall purify the sons of Levi, and purge them as gold and silver, that they may offer unto the Lord an offering in righteousness.

Then shall the offering of Judah and Jerusalem be pleasant unto the Lord, as in the days of old, and as in former years.

Many persons have supposed that John, the Baptist, was the messenger spoken of in the above prophecy, but let the reader review for a moment: The Lord did not suddenly come to his temple in the personage of Christ; he taught in the temple, but they had power to abuse him and "Cast him out;" but when the above is fulfilled "Who may abide the day of his coming and who shall be able to stand?"

The offering of Judah and Jerusalem is to be

pleasant unto the Lord as in the days of old."—
These are occurrences demanding of us more than
an ordinary thought; they have never taken place,
hence they are future.

I saw in the night visions, and, behold, one like
the Son of man came with the clouds of heaven,
and came to the Ancient of days, and they brought
him near before him.

And there was given him dominion, and glory,
and a kingdom, that all people, nations, and lan-
guages, should serve him: his dominion is an everlasting dominion, which shall not pass away, and
his kingdom that which shall not be destroyed.—
(Dan. 7:13–14).

Should times change, and Israel become as "in
former years;" then the days will be Ancient days
or like unto the ancient times;   And Daniel saw
one come with the clouds of heaven, and receive
a kingdom composed of all people and nations,
we have no account of this having taken place,
hence it must be future.

Who is this that cometh from Edom, with dyed
garments from Bozrah? this that is glorious in
his apparel, travelling in the greatness of his
strength?   I that speak in righteousness, mighty
to save.

Wherefore art thou red in thine apparel, and
thy garments like him that treadeth in the winefat!

I have trodden the winepress alone; and of the
people there was none with me: for I will tread
them in mine anger, and trample them in my fury; and their blood shall be sprinkled upon my
garments, and I will stain all my raiment.

For the day of vengeance is in mine heart, and the year of my redeemed is come.

And I looked, and there was none to help; and I wondered that there was none to uphold: therefore mine own arm brought salvation unto me; and my fury, it upheld me.

And I will tread down the people in mine anger, and make them drunk in my fury, and I will bring down their strength to the earth.

I will mention the lovingkindnesses of the Lord, and the praises of the Lord, according to all that the Lord hath bestowed on us, and the great goodness toward the house of Israel, which he hath bestowed on them according to his mercies, and according to the multitude of his lovingkindnesses.

For he said, Surely they are my people, children that will not lie: so he was their Saviour.

In all their affliction he was afflicted, and the Angel of his presence saved them: in his love and in his pity he redeemed them; and he bare them, and carried them all the days of old. (Isaiah 63: 1-9).

The various dispensations, at different times, according to the record of the past, have established the fact, that God has appointed certain times for special work to be performed on the earth. Although the time may seem long, and the persecutor's hand not withheld, and thousands of firm believers in God's promises made to bow down to Idols, yet "the day of vengeance" will come, and the year of redemption to those who worship the God of our fathers.

And the Redeemer shall come to Zion, and unto.

them that turn from transgression in Jacob, saith the Lord.

As for me, this is my covenant with them, saith the Lord; My Spirit that is upon thee, and my words which I have put in thy mouth, shall not depart out of thy mouth, nor out of the mouth of thy seed's seed, saith the Lord, from henceforth and forever.   (Isa. 59:20-21).

The Spirit spoken of in the above, will harmonize earth with heaven; be a covenant of perpetual peace; a medium by which men will be taught God's ways, giving him direct access to all Light and Truth, thereby exalting him in the kingdom of God and perfecting him for eternal life.

Behold, the day of the Lord cometh, and thy spoil shall be divided in the midst of thee.

For I will gather all nations against Jerusalem to battle; and the city shall be taken, and the houses rifled, and the women ravished; and half of the city shall go forth into captivity, and the residue of the people shall not be cut off from the city.

Then shall the Lord go forth, and fight against those nations, as when he fought in the day of battle.

And his feet shall stand in that day upon the mount of Olives, which is before Jerusalem on the east, and the mount of Olives shall cleave in the midst thereof toward the east and toward the west, and there shall be a very great valley; and half of the mountain shall remove toward the north, and half of it toward the south.

And ye shall flee to the valley of the mountains; for the valley of the mountains shall reach unto

Azal: yea, ye shall flee, like as ye fled from before the earthquake in the days of Uzziah king of Judah: and the lord my God shall come, and all the saints with thee.

*   *   *   *

And the Lord shall be King over all the earth: ❧ in that day shall there be one Lord, and his name one.

All the land shall be turned as a plain from Geba to Rimmon south of Jerusalem: and it shall be lifted up, and inhabited in her place, from Benjamin's gate unto the place of the first gate, unto the corner gate, and from the tower of Hananeel unto the king's winepresses.

And men shall dwell in it, and there shall be no more utter destruction; but Jerusalem shall be safely inhabited.

And this shall be the plague wherewith the Lord will smite all the people that have fought against Jerusalem; Their flesh shall consume away while they stand upon their feet, and their eyes shall consume away in their holes, and their tongue shall consume away in their mouth.

And it shall come to pass in that day, that a great tumult from the Lord shall be among them; and they shall lay hold every one on the hand of his neighbour, and his hand shall rise up against the hand of his neighbour.

And Judah also shall fight at Jerusalem; and the wealth of all the heathen round about shall be gathered together, gold, and silver, and apparel, in great abundance.

And so shall be the plague of the horse, of the mule, of the camel, and of the ass, and of all the beasts that shall be in these tents, as this plague.

And it shall come to pass, that every one that is

left of all the nations which came against Jerusalem, shall even go up from year to year to worship
the King, the Lord of hosts, and to keep the feast
of tabernacles.   (Zech. 14:16).

From the above prophecy we learn that a great
division of the spoil is to take place in Jerusalem;
various nations are to unite to subdue the Jewish
nation; the reckless soldiers will plunder the
houses, and abuse and outrage the women; half
of the city, only, is to go into captivity; then the
Lord appears on the mount of Olives and the
mount is cleft asunder leaving a great valley in
its place; the remaining Israelites resort, at once,
to this valley for safety; all controversy is over,
and the residue of all nations that fought against
Jerusalem are required to go up annually to worship at Jerusalem.

And at that time shall Michael stand up, the
great prince which standeth for the children of
thy people: and there shall be a time of trouble,
such as never was since there was a nation even
to that same time: and at that time thy people
shall be delivered, every one that shall be found
written in the book.

And many of them that sleep in the dust of the
earth shall awake, some to everlasting life, and
some to shame and everlasting contempt.

And they that be wise shall shine as the brightness of the firmament; and they that turn many
to righteousness, as the stars forever and ever.—
(Daniel 12:1-3).

The "trouble" that is yet to come upon Israel,

in the hour of their redemption, will, doubtless, be wonderful; but it will soon pass over, and Judah be saved forever; for He who holds the keys of death and the grave will come to his own, and fully reward them by dividing their inheritance; removing the original curse from the earth, and opening the gates to the Garden of Eden by the removing of the "Flaming Sword," once placed there to guard it, while millions of reckless soldiers and those who have persisted in persecuting God's chosen people, are confounded.

The word that Isaiah the son of Amos saw concerning Judah and Jerusalem.

And it shall come to pass in the last days, that the mountain of the Lord's house shall be established in the top of the mountains, and shall be exalted above the hills; and all nations shall flow unto it.

And many people shall go and say, Come ye, and let us go up to the mountain of the Lord, to the house of the God of Jacob; and he will teach us of his ways, and we will walk in his paths: for out of Zion shall go forth the law, and the word of the Lord from Jerusalem.

And he shall judge among the nations, and shall rebuke many people: and they shall beat their swords into ploughshares, and their spears into pruninghooks: nation shall not lift up sword against nation, neither shall they learn war any more.

O house of Jacob, come ye, and let us walk in the light of the Lord.   (Isa. 2:1-5).

The re-building of the Lord's house at Jerusalem will be done with a view to fully establish peace, not only in Israel, but among all nations. On many of the pages of this book, the Prophets have declared that God would be exalted among all people. Jehovah has plainly informed us that he would yet choose Israel and cause them to send forth the word of the Lord from Jerusalem. The word of God being His law, the nations will be required to obey it in order to abide the Millennial reign; and they must, also, cease to learn war.

For God will save Zion, and will build the cities of Judah: that they may dwell there, and have it in possession.

The seed also of his servant shall inherit it: and they that love his name shall dwell therein.—(Psalms 69 :35–36).

I was glad when they said unto me, Let us go into the house of the Lord.

Our feet shall stand within thy gates, O Jerusalem.

Jerusalem is builded as a city that is compact together:

Whither the tribes go up, the tribes of the Lord, unto the testimony of Israel, to give thanks unto the name of the Lord.

For there are set thrones of judgment, the thrones of the house of David.

Pray for the peace of Jerusalem: they shall prosper that love thee.

Peace be within thy walls, and prosperity within thy palaces.

For my brethren and companions' sakes, I will now say, Peace be within thee.

Because of the house of the Lord our God I will seek thy good.   (Psalms 102:1–9).

Then he said unto me, Son of man, these bones are the whole house of Israel: behold, they say, Our bones are dried, and our hope is lost; we are cut off for our parts.

Therefore prophesy and say unto them, Thus saith the Lord God: Behold, O my people, I will open your graves, and cause you to come up out of your graves, and bring you into the land of Israel.

And ye shall know that I am the Lord, when I have opened your graves, O my people, and brought you up out of your graves,

And shall put my spirit in you, and ye sha 1 live, and I shall place you in your own land; then shall ye know that I the Lord have spoken it, and performed it, saith the Lord.   (Ezekiel 37:11–14).

The hope of the resurrection was ancient Israel's hope: The people who lived near to God and kept his commands did not anticipate a reward until the true Messiah, or Shiloh, comes to the earth and fully establish the expected kingdom: when those who are waiting within the gates of the Paradise of God are called to take their places appointed them.   Nothing can appear more sublime than to behold the Twelve Tribes of Israel marching in perfect order, each taking its respective place, with no envious spirit pervading their breasts; When the knowledge of God fully covers the earth and the Spirit of God dwells with all flesh.

Abraham "Sought a City whose maker and

builder is God." He saw the Holy City, in a vis-
ion, as it would be finally established on the earth
The modern method of spiritualizing the word of
God, especially where it relates to the changes to
be made on this earth, will prove to be a myth to
those who may be living a few years hence. The
great day of miracles is now beginning to appear,
and will inc rease in power until Israel is established in order on the Earth.

Moses did a noble work in God's name in the
recovery of the Hebrews from a terrible bondage,
but his great achievement vanishes and is lost;
but they shall exclaim, "The Lord liveth that
brought the children of Israel from the North
Country and from all nations whither the Lord
hath driven them." Abraham, Isaac and Jacob,
together with Moses and all the Prophets, have
plainly told us that the reward of the righteous
was to be "At the time of the end. Job under-
stood this and wrote to that effect:

Oh that my words were now written! oh that
they were printed in a book!

That they were graven with an iron pen and
lead in the rock for ever!

For I know that my Redeemer liveth, and that
he shall stand at the latter day upon the earth:

And though after my skin worms destroy this
body, yet in m flesh shall I see God:

Whom I shall see for myself, and mine eyes
shall behold, and not another; though my reins
be consumed within me. (Job 19:23-27).

Abraham did not find the City he sought on earth, but will in due time.

Noah was commanded to build an ark, and he did as he was commanded, and thereby saved his famiiy. Had Noah lived, and the deluge come in our time, some of our brethren might have persuaded him that it was a spiritual ark that was demanded, and the consequence would be a lost family. Moses, also, might be induced to believe that it was simply a spiritual deliverance wanted in Egypt, and would let his brethren continue to toil in slavery and oppression. I would here remark that it is well that they lived when they did; and let us not be deceived, for we may truthfully look for a literal fulfillment of God's word in the gathering again of His people.

Blessed is the man whom thou choosest, and causest to approach unto thee, that he may dwell in thy courts: we shall be satisfied with the goodness of thy house, even of the holy temple.— (Psalms 65:4.

Wait on the Lord, and keep his way, and he shall exalt thee to inherit the land: when the wicked are cut off, thou shalt see it.

I have seen the wicked in great power, and spreading himself like a green bay tree.

Yet he passed away, and, lo, he was not: yea, I sought him, but he could not be found.

Mark the perfect man, and behold the upright: for the end of that man is peace. (Ps. 37:34-37).

When the Lord shall build up Zion, he shall appear in his glory.

He will regard the prayer of the destitute, and not despise their prayer.

This shall be written for the generation to come: and the people which shall be created shall praise the Lord.

For he hath looked down from the height of his sanctuary; from heaven did the Lord behold the earth;

To hear the groaning of the prisoner; to loose those that are appointed to death;

To declare the name of the Lord in Zion, and his praise in Jerusalem;

When the people are gathered together, and the kingdoms, to serve the Lord.   (Ps. 102:16-22).

PART THIRD.

THE CHRISTIAN'S MESSIAH.

In the First and Second Parts of this work, the prophetic evidence has been confined strictly to the ancient Scriptures: I now quote from the New Testament, to obtain evidence of an expected government or kingdom, with a governor or ruler, bearing so striking a similarity, both in his advent to the earth and his reign in the proposed nation with that of the long anticipated Messiah of the Jews, that either Jew or Greek may find in the few testimonies offered, far less difference between the hope of those who wrote the New Testament and the Jews, than is commonly supposed to exist.

And as they heard these things, he added and spake a parable, because he was nigh to Jerusalem, and because they thought that the kingdom of God should immediately appear.

He said therefore, A certain nobleman went into a far country to receive for himself a kingdom, and to return.

And he called his ten servants, and delivered them ten pounds, and said unto them, Occupy till I come.

But his citizens hated him, and sent a message after him, saying, We will not have this man to reign over us.

And it came to pass, that when he was returned,

having received the kingdom, then he commanded these servants to be called unto him, to whom
he had given the money, that he might know
how much every man had gained by trading.—
(Luke 19:11–15).

Watch therefore; for ye know neither the day
nor the hour wherein the Son of man cometh.

For the kingdom of heaven is as a man travelling into a far country, who called his own servants, and delivered unto them his goods.

And unto one he gave five talents, to another
two, and to another one; to every man according
to his several ability; and straightway took his
journey. [Mat. 25:13–15].

Luke, in the 21st chap. and 24th verse, records
the following relative to the Jewish nation:

And they shall fall by the edge of the sword,
and shall be led away captive into all nations:
and Jerusalem shall be trodden down of the Gentiles, until the times of the Gentiles be fulfilled.

History informs us that the above prediction
has been literally fulfilled; and only at the present time has the tyrant's heel been removed.

For what is a man profited, if he shall gain the
whole world, and lose his own soul? or what shall
a man give in exchange for his soul?

For the Son of man shall come in the glory of
his Father with his angels: and then he shall reward every man according to his works. [Mat.
16:26–27].

Ye are they which have continued with me in
my temptations.

And I appoint unto you a kingdom, as my
Father hath appointed unto me;

That ye may eat and drink at my table in my kingdom, and sit on thrones, judging the twelve tribes of Israel. [Luke 22:28–30].

The above confirms the testimony already offered, viz: The perpetual organization of the tribes.

O Jerusalem, Jerusalem, thou that killest the prophets, and stonest them which are sent unto thee, how often would I have gathered thy children together, even as a hen gathereth her chickens under her wings, and ye would not!

Behold, your house is left unto you desolate.

For I say unto you, Ye shall not see me henceforth, till ye shall say, Blessed is he that cometh in the name of the Lord. [Mat. 23:37–39].

When the Son of man shall come in his glory, and all the holy angels with him, then shall he sit upon the throne of his glory:

And before him shall be gathered all nations: and he shall separate them one from another, as a shepherd divideth his sheep from the goats:

And he shall set the sheep on his right hand, but the goats on the left. [Mat. 25:31–33].

Then answered Peter and said unto him, Behold, we have forsaken all, and followed thee; what shall we have therefore?

And Jesus said unto them, Verily I say unto you, That ye which have followed me, in the regeneration when the Son of man shall sit in the throne of his glory, ye also shall sit upon twelve thrones, judging the twelve tribes of Israel.

But many that are first shall be last; and the last shall be first. [Mat. 19:27–30].

When they therefore were come together, they asked of him, saying, Lord, wilt thou at this time restore again the kingdom to Israel?

And he said unto them, It is not for you to know the times or the seasons, which the Father hath put in his own power.

But ye shall receive power, after that the Holy Ghost is come upon you: and ye shall be witnesses unto me both in Jerusalem, and in all Judea, and in Samaria, and unto the uttermost part of the earth.

And when he had spoken these things, while they beheld, he was taken up; and a cloud received him out of their sight.

And while they looked steadfastly toward heaven as he went up, behold, two men stood by them in white apparel;

Which also said, Ye men of Galilee, why stand ye gazing up into heaven? this same Jesus, which is taken up from you into heaven, shall so come in like manner as ye have seen him go into heaven. [Acts 1:6–11].

So Christ was once offered to bear the sins of many; and unto them that look for him shall he appear the second time without sin unto salvation. [Hebrews 9:28].

I charge thee therefore before God, and the Lord Jesus Christ, who shall judge the quick and the dead at his appearing and his kingdom;

Preach the word; be instant in season, out of season; reprove, rebuke, exhort with all longsuffering and doctrine. [2nd Tim. 4:1–2].

For the grace of God that bringeth salvation hath appeared to all men,

Teaching us that, denying ungodliness and worldly lusts, we should live soberly, righteously, and godly, in this present world;

Looking for that blessed hope, and the glorious appearing of the great God and our Saviour Jesus Christ; [Titus 2:11–14].

I give thee charge in the sight of God, who quickeneth all things, and before Christ Jesus, who before Pontius Pilate witnessed a good confession ;

That thou keep this commandment without spot, unrebukeable, until the appearing of our Lord Jesus Christ:

When in his times he shall shew, who is the blessed and only Potentate, the King of kings, and Lord of lords; [1st Tim. 6:13-15].

But those things, which God before had shewed by the mouth of all his prophets, that Christ should suffer, he hath so fulfilled.

Repent ye therefore, and be converted, that your sins may be blotted out, when the times of refreshing shall come from the presence of the Lord ;

And he shall send Jesus Christ, which before was preached unto you :

Whom the heaven must receive until the times of restitution of all things, which God hath spoken by the mouth of all his holy prophets since the world began. [Acts 3:18-21].

And to you who are troubled rest with us, when the Lord Jesus shall be revealed from heaven with his mighty angels,

    *   *   *   *   *

When he shall come to be glorified in his saints, and to be admired in all them that believe (because our testimony among you was believed in that day. [2nd Thes. 1:7-10].

And Enoch also, the seventh from Adam, prophesied of these, saying, Behold, the Lord cometh with ten thousand of his saints,   [Jude 1:14].

Behold, he cometh with clouds; and every eye shall see him, and they also which pierced him : and all kindreds of the earth shall wail because of him. Even so, Amen. (Rev. 1:7).

For I would not, brethren, that ye should be ignorant of this mystery, (lest ye should be wise in your own conceits) that blindness in part is happened to Israel, until the fulness of the Gentiles be come in.

And so all Israel shall be saved: as it is written, There shall come out of Zion the Deliverer, and shall turn away ungodliness from Jacob:

For this is my covenant unto them, when I shall take away their sins.

As concerning the gospel, they are enemies for your sakes: but as touching the election, they are beloved for the fathers' sakes. (Rom. 10:25–28).

But I would not have you to be ignorant brethren, concerning them which are asleep, that ye sorrow not, even as others which have no hope.

For if we believe that Jesus died and rose again, even so them also which sleep in Jesus will God bring with him.

For this we say unto you by the word of the Lord, that we which are alive and remain unto the coming of the Lord shall not prevent them which are asleep.

For the Lord himself shall descend from heaven with a shout, with the voice of the archangel, and with the trump of God: and the dead in Christ shall rise first:

Then we which are alive and remain shall be caught up together with them in the clouds, to meet the Lord in the air: and so shall we ever be with the Lord. (1st Thes. 4:13–17).

And now I stand and am judged for the hope of the promise made of God unto our fathers:

Unto which promise our twelve tribes, instantly serving God day and night, hope to come. For which hope's sake, king Agrippa, I am accused of the Jews.

Why should it be thought a thing incredible with you, that God should raise the dead! (Acts 26:6-8).

Abraham was forbidden the right to settle in Palestine; God notified him that four hundred years must pass away before "The iniquity of the Amorites was full." Noah had a special mission of one hundred and twenty years, to warn the Antediluvians of their wickedness, prior to their being destroyed by water. Ninevah was warned of God's. displeasure, and the days of their probation were set. Jesus Christ warned the Jewish nation of their overthrow and their dispersion to all nations at the point of the sword.

And now the great sign is, the removal of the blindness and the restoration of the Jews to their own land from all nations, and the renewal of the covenant with them.

And there was given me a reed like unto a rod: and the angel stood, saying, Rise, and measure the temple of God, and the altar, and them that worship therein.

But the court which is witbout the temple leave out, and measure it not: for it is given unto the Gentiles: and the holy city shall they tread under foot forty and two months.

And I will give power unto my two witnesses, and they shall prophesy a thousand two hundred and threescore days, clothed in sackcloth.

These are the two olive trees, and the two candlesticks standing before the God of the earth.

And if any man will hurt them, fire proceedeth

out of their mouth, and devoureth their enemies: and if any man will hurt them, he must in this manner be killed.

These have power to shut heaven, that it rain not in the days of their prophecy: and have power over waters to turn them to blood, and to smite the earth with all plagues, as often as they will.

And when they shall have finished their testimony, the beast that ascendeth out of the bottomless pit shall make war against them, and shall overcome them, and kill them.

And their dead bodies shall lie in the street of the great city, which spiritually is called Sodom and Egypt, where also our Lord was crucified.

And they of the people and kindreds and tongues and nations shall see their dead bodies three days and a half, and shall not suffer their dead bodies to be put in graves.

And they that dwell upon the earth shall rejoice over them, and make merry, and shall send gifts one to another; because these two prophets tormented them that dwelt on the earth.

And after three days and a half the Spirit of life from God entered into them, and they stood upon their feet; and great fear fell upon them which saw them.

And they heard a great voice from heaven saying unto them, Come up hither. And they ascended up to heaven in a cloud; and their enemies beheld them.

And the same hour was there a great earthquake, and the tenth part of the city fell, and in the earthquake were slain of men seven thousand: and the remnant were affrighted, and gave glory to the God of heaven.

The second woe is past; and, behold, the third woe cometh quickly.

And the seventh angel sounded; and there were great voices in heaven, saying, The kingdoms of this world are become the kingdoms of our Lord, and of his Christ; and he shall reign for ever and ever.

    *   *   *   *   *

And the nations were angry, and thy wrath is come, and the time of the dead, that they should be judged, and that thou shouldest give reward unto thy servants the prophets, and to the saints, and them that fear thy name, small and great; and shouldest destroy them which destroy the earth. (Rev. 11:1–18).

After the building of the Temple in Jerusalem, a certain portion of it is to be measured off for the true worshippers, another portion is to be given to the Gentiles, who will trample upon the liberties of the Hebrews forty and two months, or three and a half years.

Two witnesses of the Jewish nation will be chosen of God, who will prophesy and warn all classes of men, of God's purposes concerning the earth, and like Elijah of old, they have power over the elements, which goes to prove their divine mission.   God's wrath is come, also the time for him to judge the dead and reward the prophets.

And what shall I more say? for the time would fail me to tell of Gideon, and of Barak, and of Sampson, and of Jepthah; of David also, and Samuel, and of the prophets:

Who through faith subdued kingdoms, wrought righteousness, obtained promises, stopped the mouths of lions,

Quenched the violence of fire, escaped the edge of the sword, out of weakness were made strong, waxed valiant in fight, turned to flight the armies of the aliens.

Women received their dead raised to life again: and others were tortured, not accepting deliverance; that they might obtain a better resurrection:

And others had trial of cruel mockings and scourgings, yea, moreover of bonds and imprisonment:

They were stoned, they were sawn asunder, were tempted, were slain with the sword: they wandered about in sheepskins and goatskins; being destitute, afflicted, tormented;

Of whom the world was not worthy: they wandered in deserts, and in mountains, and in dens and caves of the earth.

And these all, having obtained a good report through faith, received not the promise:

God having provided some better thing for us, that they without us should not be made perfect. (Heb. 11:32–40).

www.ingramcontent.com/pod-product-compliance
Lightning Source LLC
Chambersburg PA
CBHW021531090426
42739CB00007B/876